HOW TO KEEP THAT OTHER LADY FROM SHOWING UP!

10 Practical Parenting Tips for Mommas of Young Children

Nefertiti Harris, M.S. Ed.

I Empower, LLC

www.iempowerLLC.com

Cover design- Marqueus Draper

Photography credits- Bethany Moore

Editor- Andrea Leeth

Print ISBN: 979-8-9860915-1-8

eBook ISBN: 979-8-9860915-0-1

Printed in the United States of America

DEDICATION

I dedicate this book to one of my angels in heaven, my oldest son, Lamonté. May his soul be at peace.

To my four other children, Donniesha, Elora, Neriah, and Donaldo, Jr., may you always know just how much I love you!

To my husband, Donaldo, Sr., thank you for the beautiful family we have created together.

To my mom and dad, thank you for your beautiful example of parenting.

TABLE OF CONTENTS

PREFACE

Have you ever felt that parenting was hard?

Have you been at the point of feeling like
you do not know what to do?

Parenting can be challenging and even stressful at
times! But everyday does not have to be that way.

First, congratulations on purchasing this book. In my opinion, parenting is the most important job, and it does not come with a manual or training. So, kudos to you for seeking ways to develop yourself as a parent! Or maybe you received this book as a present. Well, whoever gifted it to you must know that you are the type of momma who takes your role seriously and is always looking for ways to become even better!

However you may have acquired this book, I hope that your family is blessed by the tips and words of encouragement that fill these pages. They were written with YOU and your kiddos in mind, so glean from it what you think will work for you and your family and be intentional with the implementation.

If you are anything like me, then you have experienced a time or two in your walk as a momma that you are not proud of. It may have been a time when you yelled, and it felt necessary at the time, but later, after reflecting, you realized that you could have handled the situation better. Or maybe you didn't yell, but you reacted in a way that made your kid(s) feel bad. The specifics of your situation may differ, but however you may relate, I believe we would agree that those are moments that we wish we could take back.

Overtime, I began referring to my "not-so-proud moments" as "That OTHER lady." You know that lady who you revert to when you are feeling stressed and when your kids do not seem to hear what you are saying (No matter how many times you have said it). That lady that you try your best to not allow your guests to see. The lady who you really may be working to erase. Or the lady who you may earnestly want to change. If we are truly honest, we can all admit that at one point or another, THAT lady seems to surface. This book is designed to give you tips to help keep that OTHER lady in check!

(Although I poke fun at it, if you find yourself in a situation where that OTHER lady is not a joke, then please seek help from a friend, loved one, or a professional).

What this book is not!

This book is NOT a one-size-fits-all approach to parenting. Our family units are way too diverse for us to think that one style or one method is going to be best for everyone.

It is also not POOF! Magic! ... that if used, will suddenly make all your stress go away and turn you into the perfect mom. If anyone finds that method, I think we all would be lined up to get the big secret. The truth is, being a parent is a blessing, and there are days that sometimes feel super-overwhelming, and there are other days when you feel like you hit a homerun, touchdown, or made the winning three-pointer shot! Do not worry, that will be the extent of my sports analogies. I am not a huge sports mom, but I must be in touch a little bit because I have sons who love sports, so it helps us to connect.

What this book is!

What you can expect from this book are real, practical things that I have done with my own children and for the many children who I have had the pleasure of taking care of for over twenty-five years. I will share with you the things that have helped me to become the type of mom that I really want to be, and the techniques that I have incorporated into our lives to keep the OTHER lady under wraps, and eventually ... hopefully, get to the point when she does not have to surface at all.

Now, don't get me wrong, and hear me clearly, we all must keep a little "momma bear" close by for the times when we have to go into protection mode for our little or not-so-little ones. That motherly instinct, and the "I will ALWAYS have your back" mentality, is ... with no apologies ... definitely a keeper! The OTHER lady, however, is a little different, she is not always rational, and sometimes we allow her to say and do things that make our kids feel not so great, which if we are honest also makes us feel not so great as well.

What I hope you will gather from these tips is that if you are a bit more proactive instead of reactive, your days with your little ones can be more enjoyable and less stressful. Remember, there is no cut and dry science to parenting. As you gain experience and grow, you will also gain wisdom. You will keep some practices and may decide to change up some things as the years go by. You may also see that some techniques work better with some children than others. Many of us have seen this with our own parents who do things differently with their grandchildren. I have heard parents say, "Well, we did not know any better so we did the best we could." I think we would all, or at least MOST of us, agree that as mothers that is what we do … the best that we know how to do.

In this book, I will share with you ten tips from my "toolbox" or "fanny pack" (Yes, I do occasionally use a fanny pack, and I am not ashamed to admit it)! In many situations, I find it quite useful for keeping my hands free. But in this instance, I am not talking about an actual toolbox or fanny pack, but rather I am referring to my stash of tips and strategies that I pull out and use in my daily parenting. If I find that one is not working, I simply switch it out for another. So, without any further ado, let us dive in!

TIP #1
LOOK IN THE MIRROR!

As mothers, we often parent just like our parents or the complete opposite. Maybe you have heard the story of two siblings growing up in the same home with a parent who was an alcoholic. One of the siblings becomes an alcoholic just like their parent, and the other one never drinks a day in his or her life because they vowed to never be like THAT parent.

It all comes down to a decision or series of decisions that YOU make daily. I do recognize that there are some things in life that happen that we have no control over. However, there are many things that you DO have control over and those are the things that I am encouraging you to focus on and recognize the level of power that you truly possess.

Take a moment to reflect on, and jot down, your responses to the following questions:

1) Are you currently parenting the way you have always dreamed to parent? List some things that you like about

your parenting style and list some things that come to mind that you might want to work on changing. Don't skip this part and say you will do it later (yes, I know how we do as mommas). Go ahead, jot your answers down now.

____

____

____

____

____

____

____

____

____

____

2) Overall, are you proud of your parenting? List some of your proud parenting moments below (even if you have answered that you are not overall proud. Find a moment or two and jot them down below).

As mothers, we LOVE to share those proud parenting moments and rightfully so. Be sure to recognize the areas and the moments in which you are rocking it as a mom! Be mindful of your own self-talk and keep it positive. On the days that you feel like you are not "winning," it is important to have a trusted friend or family member who you can lean on. That friend needs to be able to tell you to pull yourself together if you are being irrational or be willing and able to just LISTEN as you vent! Many times, as moms, we feel better after we let off some steam and just get it off our chest. I am sure you are familiar with the saying, "It takes a village to raise children," so I encourage you to tap into your village!

I have asked you to reflect on the previous questions because YOU can choose to be the type of parent that YOU want to be! You do not have to do what your parents did or anyone else around you for that matter. Even if, to this day, you are not happy with the way you have parented your children, you can choose to be different from here on out. If you are changing your parenting style or some of your techniques, it will take more effort on your part, especially depending on the age of your children, but I am a firm believer of the adage, "When you know better, you do better!" So, I say, stop making excuses, and instead, make a decision and stick with it! As we will discuss later, consistency is going to be a key factor in your success.

Lastly, don't compare yourself or your kids to other people. Stop looking at social media thinking, "I wish my kids were like so-and-so's kids, etc." Remember, people only post what they want you to know. You never truly know what goes on in their homes unless you are front, center, and present. Even then, the family may act differently when they have guests.

So, momma, it is time to get your mind right! As you read through this book, continuously reflect on your own practices. My hope is that by the end of this book, you will identify some key areas that you need to address within your family, and you will begin to implement the strategies that you feel will work best for you and your kids. Also, do not forget about your parenting wins! There may also be some things that I describe in this book that you are already doing. That is a parenting win for you. Well, as they say, "Great minds think alike," so kudos to you for being ahead of the game!

The Gist:

You do not have to parent just like your parents.

You can choose to be the type of parent
YOU desire to be!

Identify a trusted friend or family member
to lean on in difficult times.

TIP # 2
UNDERSTAND, KIDS
ARE PEOPLE TOO

I have never been a fan of the parenting style that says, "I am the parent, and my kids should do what I say and that is just that!" Do not get me wrong, there is a time and place for that mentality especially when there is an emergency or danger. However, to simply never let a child feel empowered or feel like their feelings or opinions matter, just does not work well for me as a parent. I do, however, believe that not everything in life or with parenting is up for negotiations.

I remember one day when my daughter was a toddler, I was driving, and she kept calling me or saying something from the backseat. I remember getting frustrated, and I yelled at her. I looked at her in the rearview mirror, and I saw how her facial expression changed. I will never forget that moment or the look on her face. It seemed like I had crushed her spirit, and I felt horrible about it. I can only imagine how she felt at that moment. Thankfully, kids are very forgiving, and to my knowledge, she does not remember this incident at all, but it did make me reflect on my reaction. Really, who enjoys having someone yell at them? Honestly, no one that I know would say that they do.

To this day, I distinctly remember working a summer job as a receptionist for a real estate firm in Manhattan, and one of the executives called upset because his car had not arrived to pick him up. He then proceeded to yell at me, and in that moment, I was so shaken that I was almost brought to tears. The fact that I still remember that incident today, shows how much I do not like for anyone to yell at me, and I try to keep that in mind when I interact with my children as well.

So, does that OTHER lady rear her ugly head at times? Yes, she does, and when she does, I am not afraid to own up, admit where I went wrong, and apologize to my kids. Yes, I do believe that parents should apologize when they are wrong.

Our words are powerful, and we have such a great influence over our children. So, before you react to a situation, pause, and ask yourself, how would you feel if someone said what you are about to say to you? Or if they did what you were about to do to you? It truly is the Golden Rule in action, "Do unto others as you would have done unto you." If this is taught to children, and it is cool for us to use with our adult interactions, then why should we treat our kids any differently? **Remember, kids are just little people who have feelings, and a voice just like we do as adults.**

Kids should respect their parents, and parents should also respect their kids. I believe as mommas, you should acknowledge, validate, and respect their feelings. This does not at all mean that as mommas, we should allow them to do whatever they feel or desire to do (more will be discussed on this in a later tip).

The Gist:

Kids are people too!

Remember the Golden Rule.

Admit and apologize when you are wrong.

TIP #3
FUN! MAKE IT FUN

I remember one night, we had a long day with work and school, and I was tired and did not have the energy to cook. So, on a whim, I decided we were going to have a Cereal Party!!! My youngest daughter, who seriously did not even like cereal at the time, even joined in! She even did so happily! I presented it with such ENTHUSIASM that I won her over! Presentation is EVERYTHING!

To be honest, I was amazed as I watched it unfold. I remember thinking, "Wow, this is really working." We made it a big deal. We dragged one of their little kid tables into mom and dad's room, where we got to eat. We had options of toppings like chocolate chips, granola, and nuts that we added into the cereal. We added some fruit as a side, put on some music and BAM! We had dinner and a party! Now, some key factors to my kid's reception to what I was saying was my energy and enthusiasm. How you present any idea and the energy you give off, be it positive or negative, will impact how your kids receive and respond to what you are saying. I would like to clarify that we do not have cereal parties every week, but you know what, we all ate that night and made it a fun evening!

You might be thinking, I do not have the energy to do all of that. Well look at it this way, would you rather exert the energy yelling and fussing with your kids, or would you rather use that energy in a positive manner that leaves both you and them feeling joyful and positive in the end? I imagine most of you would want the latter situation.

Be silly with your kids! Create traditions that they look forward to doing every so often. To this day, my kids and I still sing and sometimes dance to our made up "Friday" song. Here are the lyrics:

It's Friday, It's Friday, oh yeah, oh yeah!

No school tomorrow, no school tomorrow, oh yeah, oh yeah!

We get to sleep in, we get to sleep in, oh yeah, oh yeah!

Then it continues with anyone adding in their own verse! The ending changes all the time! It makes us laugh and adds so much joy to the moment.

Now, I am a teacher, so by no means is our Friday song an "anti-school" message. I think my kids get a kick out of me being excited and celebrating the fact that there is no school on Saturday, and we get to sleep in. Hey, we all need a break sometimes. I just choose to let them see that I relate to their feelings as well.

I love having fun with my kids. They know, however, that when I mean business, I mean business. I often remind them of that also. I establish clear boundaries with my kids. So, I joke and play around a lot, but I am **intentional** in making sure that when we joke, it is not borderline disrespectful. If their actions or words ever cross the lines of respect, then I take the time to address it **immediately**. I do not encourage or play off their behavior, even if there are others present. I simply pull them to the side and address the matter at hand one-on-one with them, right when it happens, or if something prevents that, then shortly thereafter.

From my experience when disrespect is ignored, for whatever reason, the situation gets worse over time. Every parent has their own level of tolerance, but I encourage you to reflect on what behaviors you allow, and how it impacts your family unit. As I mentioned above, I do believe that kids should be able to express their feelings, however, I also believe that it is my job as their mom to teach them respectful ways to express themselves.

The Gist:

Get creative and make it fun!

Enjoy the parenting ride!

Keep the fun respectful and address any disrespect immediately!

TIP #4
SET THE EXPECTATIONS - FOR LIFE

As the mother or parent, I believe that it is our responsibility to teach our children the expectations that we have for their behavior, and that OTHERS in various settings will also have for their behavior. Does it mean that they will always follow the guidelines? Of course not, but that does not mean that we do not do our duty and teach them.

For example, if you allow your kids to yell at you, then you are teaching them that it is okay to yell at adults. They will then go to school and think it is okay to yell at their teacher and eventually go to work thinking it is okay to yell at their boss. These actions do have a domino effect.

Here's another example. In my home, I am okay with my kids running in the house as long as they are careful of the furniture edges, etc. However, not everyone is okay with that, so it is up to me to explain that possible difference to my children. If they go to someone else's house, they will know not to run around on the inside, unless they are told by the adult that it is okay.

Kids will inevitably be faced with scenarios in which things their friends do are not in alignment with your family's expectations. In these instances, it is very helpful to explain that "in our family, we do (<u>insert behavior</u>) even though others may accept different behavior." As the parent, I encourage you to be the one to tell your child that people around them may act differently and reassure them that you trust them to do what they know is right based on our family values.

It is also important to set clear expectations for their behavior, and you, as the parent, must stick with what you say. If you give in and are inconsistent, you are teaching them by your actions, that what you say does not carry weight. Oftentimes, if my children ask for something or ask if we can do something, and I have not decided, then my response will be "maybe." That way, I have not said yes or no, so if we end up not being able to do what they requested, they will not feel like I lied because I didn't commit to it. Therefore, my word, which is important to me, does not lose its value. In all honesty, my kids do not like the "maybe" response, but I still stick to this so that my word does not lose its value.

Another example of setting expectations would be before you go in a store, decide if you will or will not allow your kids to buy something then, tell them before you get out of the vehicle or before you enter the store. Do not wait until they see something that they want to decide if they can buy it. This helps to avoid issues in the store. Of course, there will always be exceptions to the rules, but if you end up having more exceptions than sticking with the plan, you risk coming across as inconsistent and your kids will not know what to expect.

Lastly, in our home, it is important that we all feel a sense of responsibility to care for our home. I, therefore, think that kids should have chores or should have some level of responsibility for helping the household run. We encourage our kids to start by simply cleaning up after themselves. We also teach them that sometimes it is okay to clean up something that you did not actually mess up to help the entire household. Depending on the age of your children, you may decide to create a chart or checklist to help them stay organized and remember their responsibilities.

The specific tasks or chores that you give your children should be age appropriate and will be up to you to decide, but since they are all members of the home, they should feel some ownership and responsibility.

This creates a feeling that our home is just that ... OUR home, so we are all responsible for keeping it clean and presentable.

Involving your children with the upkeep of your home will also help you as a mom not feel overburdened with having to do all the cleaning by yourself. It is yet another way to keep that OTHER lady from surfacing. **After all, if we are honest, that other lady typically appears when we are feeling stressed, overworked, or when we feel a lack of support from our family members.**

The Gist:

Set clear expectations for your kids.

Be consistent and follow through with
the expectation you set.

Create a culture of ownership
and responsibility within your home.

TIP #5
USE BEHAVIOR MODIFICATION
- IF NEEDED

I remember a season of life when I had to get my younger three children up for school and day care in the morning before going to work. On many days, I was EXHAUSTED by the time I got to work. I felt drained! My mornings were the most stressful time of my day, and the fact that my time management skills were not the best, did not help the situation at all. It all added to my stress because I would then end up rushing my little people and that would cause them to stress as well.

I knew there had to be a better way! Surely, this was not how I was planning to live the rest of my life. So, what I learned over time is that I had to give myself a little extra time and prepare as much as possible the night before.

For the kid who was just like me, I knew I had to wake her up ten to fifteen minutes earlier than her siblings because she needed that extra time in the morning. Instead of rushing her when we were trying to get out the house, waking her up a little earlier gave her the extra few minutes that she required. This is still true to this day.

Since I have the background of being a classroom teacher, I decided to mix in some of the things I would do in my classroom at home. I created a chart that listed all the things my kids had to do in the morning to get ready for school and out of the house on time. I then laminated the chart and left a space for all five days of the week. For every task that they completed and checked off, they earned a point. I even included a space for bonus points that I would give out spontaneously for something that they did well that morning that was not listed on the chart.

I kept the charts and a whiteboard marker in a space near their bedrooms, and it was their responsibility to check off the chart in the morning. These charts worked like a charm! When I would go to wake up my kids, if they gave me a hard time getting out of bed, I would remind them that they would not earn their point, if they did not get up. You would be amazed at how their little heads would pop up when I reminded them of the point.

As a part of the system, once they earned a point, I could not take it away.

I make it a point to say that last part because over the years, I have seen where parents allow kids to earn something and then the minute the child makes a poor choice, the parent takes away what they earned when the two situations did not have anything to do with one another. So, if my son earned a point for making his bed, but when we pull up to school, we realize he left his bookbag at home, and he is now not prepared for school, I am not going to take away his points because I am now frustrated with him. In this instance, making his bed has nothing to do with whether he brought his bookbag. If the latter (not bringing his bookbag) warrants a consequence in your home, it should be separate from anything he has already earned. If you want my opinion, the natural consequence of not having his materials may prove to be enough.

For two years straight, my kids earned points that did not have a tangible reward. It became a joke with my husband and coworker when my husband asked, "What do the kids get for the points?" To which I quietly replied, "Please do not ask that question. They have not asked, and therefore, the reward is simply, the point!"

A great deal of being successful with this type of system is in HOW you present and execute the plan. You must make earning a point a big deal and acknowledge when they do well. When they do not earn a point or whatever you chose to call it, then you stick to it, but do not make them feel bad about it. You simply say that tomorrow is another day, and we will try again.

I know that many parents do not like or support methods that employ extrinsic, or external, rewards. If this does not suit your style, then pull out another tip from the toolbox. Remember, there is no one-stop approach to parenting. Also, please understand that my children do not always earn something tangible for their actions. I make it a point to discuss the fact that sometimes we do things because it is the right thing to do, we want to do it, or because it will help someone else.

The Gist:

Use a behavior modification plan,
IF and when you need it.

All plans do not have to include a tangible reward.

TIP #6
ACCEPT YOUR KIDS AS INDIVIDUALS

Allow your children to do the things that they love and find ways to nurture those things. Do not force things upon your kids that you wish you did, but for whatever reason, you did not. This is not a remake of your childhood. If there are similarities, then great! If not, it really is okay!

Allow your children to have some choices in what they do. Do not get me wrong, yes, you are the momma and that carries weight. There will be times when your kids need to do what you say simply because you said it. But I am not one with the belief that you should parent with an ironclad fist. Kids like to feel like they have some power. You could easily present options to your kids (all of which are acceptable to you and then allow them to choose). For example, if it is cold and they need to wear a jacket, you could say, would you like to wear the black or red jacket today? This way, they have some choice, but you ultimately are getting what you want, which is for them to wear a jacket.

Have you ever heard any of the following sayings?

- You attract more bees with honey than with vinegar?

- Kind words are like honey—sweet to the soul and healthy for the body. Proverbs 16:24

- A **gentle** answer turns away wrath, but a harsh word stirs up anger. Proverbs 15

Well, remember what I said earlier, kids are people too! So, these sayings should also apply to our interactions with our kids.

I remember one day, I was burning a candle, and the wick was kind of short. As it burned, I watched how the light began to dim as the wax around it grew and collected. The wax was smothering the light. I then picked up the glass that the candle was in, and I moved it around so that the wax spread out and gave the wick room. The flame immediately began to grow. I share this because it is the same with raising our kids. We should not smother our kids. As mommas, we need to be there to support, teach, and guide them, but still give them room to grow, shine, and learn from some of their own life lessons.

We often show others love based upon the way we like to be loved. However, our kids are not us! So, instead, pay attention to the way they express their love, and how they need you to show them love. I would first start by telling your children that you love them and say it OFTEN! I have had to pay attention to the diverse needs of my kids in their way of expressing and receiving love.

Some of my children are very touchy and love to give hugs ... even if I may not feel up to it, I put their needs before mine at that moment. After all, I would rather that they seek that hug from me than anyone else.

My kids like to tell me specific details about games, sports, YouTube channels, etc. so I listen and ask questions because that is what they like, even if I do not know much about the game, sport, or YouTuber. It is a great opportunity for my children to teach me! Believe me, they do enjoy that.

Lastly, some of my children are very sensitive and do not like to feel like they have disappointed anyone, so I am extra cognizant, I pay closer attention to what I say, what others say to them, and how they deliver what they say.

The Gist:

Don't try to live through your kids.

Give your kids choices and allow them to make decisions, when appropriate.

Love each kid how they need to be loved.

TIP #7
LEAD/PARENT BY EXAMPLE

I try my best to not parent in a way that makes me hypocritical. Have you ever found yourself, (or have witnessed others)—in case you do not wish to admit it (smile)—in any of the following situations?

Situation #1

Kid #1 comes crying to you because he or she was hit by Kid #2. Kid #2 has an elaborate explanation for why he or she hit the sibling or denies it completely. Well, as a reaction, Kid #2 gets a spanking or a hand tap and then is told, "We do not hit in this family." Or "We do not hit people we love," or simply no explanation at all.

Situation #2

Kid #1 and Kid #2 are yelling and arguing from their bedrooms. As a reaction, the parent replies by yelling above them and telling them to stop yelling at one another.

I know reading this on paper makes it seem silly, but if we were truly honest with ourselves, many of us could identify with one or both scenarios at some point in our years of parenting. In both situations, if you look at it honestly, the parent is being a hypocrite and setting double standards. One in which the parent is saying do what I say, not as I do!

I am not one in favor of spanking my kids, however, I do not judge parents that choose to spank. I do, however, believe that there are more effective ways of discipline that do not involve spanking. I think this is one of those areas that if we pause for a moment, we may see that we resort to spanking out of an emotional reaction when we are feeling frustrated. In those moments, it is probably best to walk out of the room, go into the bathroom for a moment, and just calm ourselves down before we react and discipline our kids. I honestly believe that oftentimes, kids that are spanked just become immune to it.

I have heard people say that they agree with spanking because of the verse "spare the rod, spoil the child." Well, again, I believe that the rod does not have to be physical. It could simply represent discipline. The verse is therefore stating that discipline is important (to which, I completely agree).

I do believe that sometimes, the natural consequences of our kids' actions are enough to teach them a lesson. There does not always have to be a punishment or consequence put upon them by the parent. For example, if the child stayed up in their room after mom said go to bed, then in the morning, they will be tired and will still have to go to school.

I like to involve my kids, when appropriate, in what they think is an appropriate consequence for their actions. Often you will see that they are harder on themselves than you would have actually been. You could then take their suggestions and make the final decision. Whatever decision you make, be sure to stick with it so that you are consistent, and your child will know what to expect. Ask your kid, was that a good choice? What would you do differently if you could do it all over? Remind them that you expect them to make better choices.

Tell your kids when you are proud of them! Make sure you have one-on-one time with each kid occasionally. It does not have to be a huge all-out planned event—although it could be if that is what you decide. In the end, your child should feel special and know that you, as their parent, make time for them.

I do not claim to be a perfect parent. I actually do not think a perfect parent exists. I do, however, choose to parent in a way in which I am reflective and want to be better. There will be days when you feel like you should have earned a star for your role as a parent. YES! Kudos to you! As mommas, we all have those days when we feel like things are going great, and we made good choices as a parent. I also know firsthand that the opposite is true. There are days/moments that if we were being graded as a parent, we would not score very well. We all have days when you may get frustrated ... even with yourself for the way you reacted to a situation or sometimes you may wish you could turn back the hands of time to change your own behavior. I believe that as long as you reflect on your parenting and adjust as needed, you will continue to grow as a momma.

The Gist:

Be a parent of "do as I do, not simply do as I say."

Reflect on your parenting often.

TIP #8
INSTITUTE "QUIET TIME"

When my kids were about to start kindergarten, I had to begin weaning them off of taking a nap during the day. I then decided to institute a quiet time.

Here were our three basic Quiet Time rules:

1) Quiet time lasted for one hour or one and a half hours (about the time they used to nap).

2) They could not have electronics or play with one another. It was quiet time. I provided them with PLENTY of crafting items, paint, coloring books, books to read, toys, etc. They were encouraged to use their imagination.

3) If there was an emergency, then they could come and let me know. Otherwise, they stayed in their individual spaces and entertained themselves.

This was my time to get things done, have a break, or even have some quiet time with my husband. You might ask, why are the kids not allowed to play with one another during this time? Well, because that would mean they might argue, fight, be loud, etc., and what time is it? Quiet Time. In my opinion, this builds discipline, and it encourages them to be creative. They had tons of things that they could do with their time!

Again, as a common theme throughout this book, how your kids receive the concept of quiet time will heavily depend on how you present it to them. Quiet Time was not and is not a punishment ... not at all, so PLEASE do not present it as such! If you do, they will resist it, and you will create problems for yourself. Also, quiet time does not mean they could not make any sounds in their room ... I am not militant, it just means, they would play quietly by themselves.

It is a good idea to schedule quiet time instead of resorting to it when you are stressed. If you resort to it when you are upset, you will probably not present it in a positive manner, and again, it will not be received in a positive manner. In our house, we would have quiet time on Saturdays. Do what works for your family! You also have to decide at what age quiet time is appropriate for your kids. Remember, quiet time in my home began after they were no longer taking naps because they were starting kindergarten, so they were about five years old when we started instituting a quiet time.

Now that my kids are a little older, they have time that they are allowed to use their electronic devices, and then there are times when I limit their use. This is another area where I used little charts which they can self-monitor the time they spend on these devices. Yes, it does require that they are honest, which is another thing that our kids hear and see me practice. They have heard the story of *The Boy Who Cried Wolf* many times. Nowadays, there are apps that will monitor screen time for you. So, if you do not want your kids to self-monitor their time, you could use an app for that instead.

The Gist:

Create quiet time for your kids.

Schedule the quiet time.

Provide or create many (nonelectronic)
options for their quiet time.

TIP #9
SPEAK POSITIVELY OF THEM AND TO THEM

One of the things high on the list of hurting my heart is when someone says their kid is bad! STOP it! Please! This is especially worse when it is done in front of the child.

If you say your kid is bad, then I believe that you are speaking negativity into their lives. Kids are not bad. They may make poor choices at times, but hey, we all do that at times. Our poor choices should not brand us as being bad people!

Have you ever done something, openly or privately, that you later wished you had not done? Have you ever done it again even after you said you wouldn't? I will be the first to raise my hand on that one! So, again, this goes back to what I stated earlier, kids are people too, so why do we hold them up to standards or expectations that we fail to meet ourselves? This is just some food for thought.

For the most part, (there are always exceptions), I believe that kids do what you allow them to do. If you laugh when your toddler hits you, then you have just taught your child that it is okay to hit mommy, and not only is it okay, but they actually get a reward (laughter) for doing so.

It often amazes me when parents say their kids are out of control later in life, but they allowed these behaviors early on. Well, those early years count! They are actually critical foundational years when you are laying the groundwork for their behavior for years to come. Again, I believe that if you are recognizing poor choices that you allowed early on, it is not too late to get back on track, just understand that it will take more effort and consistency on your part to reteach your kids.

To this day, I will quickly correct ANYONE, including loving family members and friends, who speak negatively of my kids. Often it is stated from a pure place, and I am sure they do not mean any harm, but it is my job as their mom to speak up for them.

If your kids hear you say they are bad, and you allow others to say they are bad, then why would they act any differently? Can you imagine the thoughts that would go on in their mind when they are faced with decisions to make? I can imagine that they may think, "Well, mom says I am bad, and so-and-so says I am bad, so it must be true." I would prefer the opposite to be true, that "Mom says I have greatness inside of me, that I am a hard worker, and I can do anything I set my mind to do." Even as I typed that statement, I felt a surge of positivity rise within me. Imagine what it can do for your kids.

You must be the voice of love in your kid's life and their advocate. So, if your child makes a poor choice, you teach them to own up to it, take responsibility, and then go on from there.

The Gist:

Be mindful of the words you speak to
and about your kids.

Choose to make your voice and words uplifting.

Don't allow others to speak negativity
over your children.

TIP #10
SPREAD POSITIVITY IN YOUR HOME

I have often found that on many days, my emotions, when I begin my day, can set the tone for the emotions of other members in the house as well. When I am purposeful and intentional about the energy I give off, it makes for a better day for us all. I will admit, it does sometimes feel like extra work on my part, but when I see the positive ripple effect that it has on my children, it makes the extra worth it! The following are several suggestions for how you can add joy to your home and spread some positivity:

1. Leave your kids a positive note in their room or somewhere in the home where they can easily find it. It does not have to be fancy. If they are too young to read, you could draw them a simple picture that will make them smile.

2. Have one-on-one conversations with them to let them know that you see the good that they have been doing, even if sometimes you do not recognize them for it immediately.

3. Tell them you love them. And say it often!

4. At dinner or anytime when the whole family is together, intentionally say something positive about them or acknowledge something that they did that you appreciated. If you have multiple kids, say something positive about each of them from time to time.

5. Thank them for doing things or saying things that help the entire family. This is also great to do with your spouse, but I'll save that for another book.

This positivity is contagious, and it truly warms my heart to see it in action. I remember one day when my teenage son spontaneously left the family a message in the kitchen about love (see picture). From time to time, one of my daughters will leave me a note on my desk so that I will see it in the morning before I begin my workday. I often get random uplifting text messages from my oldest daughter, and my youngest son and daughters are great at randomly saying "I love you" or giving me an unexpected hug. In all these examples, I did not tell them to do what they did, however, these, or similar acts of kindness, were witnessed or experienced by them. Those positive actions, in turn, rubbed off on them.

Isn't that one of our ultimate goals as a parent? We want our children to, on their own, choose to exhibit behaviors and make choices that show they have been listening over the years to what we have taught them or modeled for them through our own actions. When they internalize these positive behaviors and choose to act on it themselves, it is a huge proud parenting moment!

The Gist:

Positive acts are contagious.

Be intentional about spreading positivity.

If you use these ten tips throughout your journey as a parent, they will help you keep that OTHER lady under wraps. This will in turn, make for "A BLISSSFUL" (with an extra "s") parenting experience (you can use the phrase to help you remember all ten tips). See below for a recap of the tips in the order of the "A BLISSSFUL" acronym.

THE 10 TIPS IN REVIEW

Accept your kids as individuals.

Behavior modification.

Lead and parent by example.

Institute a Quiet Time.

Set the expectations.

Speak positively to and of them.

Spread positivity.

Fun.

Understand, kids are people too.

Look in the mirror.

A BLISSSFUL parenting experience!

I hope that as you continue your journey as a parent, you will revisit this book and the ideas presented within these pages as needed. I would love to hear your success stories.

To check out some of my other work, visit my website at http://iempowerllc.com and follow us on Facebook (I Empower, LLC)!

ABOUT THE AUTHOR

Nefertiti Harris is a wife, mom, educational specialist, and entrepreneur. She has five beautiful children and one adorable granddaughter. She was born and raised in Brooklyn, NY and later moved to Virginia to attend college. She has a Master of Science in Education and a Bachelor of Science in Interdisciplinary Studies with a concentration in Elementary Education and a minor in Spanish. After getting married, she moved to Florida and now resides in Mississippi with her husband and children. Nefertiti is the CEO of I Empower, LLC and the Founder of the educational nonprofit, Uplifting Arms, Inc. Her passion is to help others and equip them with knowledge that will change their lives and help them to, in turn, change the lives of others with whom they interact.